Ode to Chores

THE GOOD, THE BAD AND THE LAUNDRY

Brenda Kahn

South Salem | New York

Copyright © 2018 by Brenda Kahn

All rights reserved. No part of this publication may be reproduced, distributed or transmitted in any form or by any means, without prior written permission.

Cover Illustration, Creative Commons CC0, redrawn by Doan Trang
Cover Design by Brenda Kahn

Ode to Chores: The Good, The Bad, and the Laundry
Brenda Kahn, 1st ed.

ISBN 978-0-9980476-0-7

South Salem Press
www. SouthSalemPress.com

ALSO BY BRENDA KAHN

Albums

Seven Laws of Gravity

Hunger

Outside the Beauty Salon

Destination Anywhere

Epiphany in Brooklyn

Goldfish Don't Talk Back

Music for Kids

Rocket to the Moon

PREFACE

Dear Someone's Mom,

    Whether you're a savvy mom of teens or a new mom trying to get baby to sleep, this book is for you. I wrote this book because I love you and no one tells you the real story of parenting until of course, the dog is eating cat poop while you're trying to warm up a bottle while your older children bite their siblings; or similar.

    I've written these poems while waiting at the doctor's office, on lunch break from one of several part time jobs, weekend mornings while everyone else was sleeping, at soccer games, and in between pick-ups and drop-offs. I suggest you read these poems in the same way. This book is also excellent bedside reading for those nights when you need a little extra empathy at the end of the day. I'm here for you.

    xo,
    Bren

*God could not be everywhere,
and therefore he made mothers*
— Rudyard Kipling

Why I Wrote This Book

I wrote this book because I was lonely. I spent hours every day with my little kids, which I really loved for a while, but my husband was gone A LOT, and when he came home, he was all talked out. He just wanted to spend a little time with his two boys roughhousing and eating Oreo Thins.

Plans with friends were few and far between because we were all busy shuffling kids to school and activities when we weren't working jobs, or doing house projects, or stumping for our chosen elected officials, or reconnecting with our significant others.

In the meantime, exhausted at the end of every day, I still wanted to be an artist, a writer, and a musician. I'd been on stage for 25 years and suddenly the only singing I was doing was lullabies at 3 AM in a rocking chair trying to get my little muffin to sleep. . . just for a little while. . . sleep muffin, sleep.

Somewhere along the way, I put down my pen and found myself deep in the stuff of kids. Then, one evening after an especially frustrating dinner with the boys, I sent everyone off to their rooms, flipped over an envelope lying in the mess on the dining room table, and wrote the poem *Stop Rocking on the Chair*. I was surprised how satisfying it was to say it on the page.

From there I started writing these "mom poems" all the time. As I did, I felt less and less alone. I was not only writing about my experience, but a thread of experience that connected to moms all over the world and through time. The common language of motherhood reconnected me to my creativity and other people at the same time.

I first thought I wrote this book for myself, but it turns out I wrote this book for you. I hope it brings you joy and even makes you cry. I hope it brings mothers together and inspires you to make some art and put it out into the world, so we can all have a moment of connection together. Call me. We'll have coffee.

Acknowledgements

To Thomas, my person
Thank you for reminding me that every moment is a building block to the arc of our time here.

To Mason, my son
Thank you for telling us to watch out for rhinos. I've seen a few. And for your keen perspective as a young adult.

To Dylan, my son
Thank you for your passion for exotic pets, spice potions, and life. And, for rocking on the chair.

Doan Trang, *thank you* for a brilliant job with the redraw of the cover art.

Elisa Karp, *thank you* for your insightful edits.

Special Thanks to my Patreon Supporters
Your support is in the binding, the pages, the font, the cover art, the production fees, and the inspiration to create. *Thank you!*

Nancy Adzentoivich, Phil Arnold, Mike Black, Steve Carotenuto, Lorne Dixon, Thomas Droge, Michael Hacker, Arlene Kahn, Kate Matthew, Jim McGuire, Scott Owen, Stuart Ross, Liz Schiller, Anne Soffee, Stacy Steele, Glen Torbert, John Wigger, and Matthew Wilson

For Mason and Dylan

Contents

MOM 1
   Ode to Chores 2
   Mom Interrupted 6
   Pale Pink House Haiku 8
   Middle Age 9
   Valentine's Day 11
   Tread Lightly Through That Fountain of Youth 13
   Today, I Shouldered Distance 15
   Dirty Socks 18
   Day Lily 20
   Mom Agrees to a Pet 21
   Time Stream 25
   Terra Madre 27
   Sweater Weather 31
   The Rhetorical Housewife 33
   The Whole of Me 34
   The Movie of My Life 35

KIDS 37
   Reluctant Reader 38
   Marvel Heroes 40
   Art Collector 41
   For the Love of Pete! *(Stop Rocking on the Chair)* 42
   Soccer Haiku 43
   What They Don't Tell You 44
   Little Toes 47
   Little Toes II 49

- Roy G Biv 50
- Common Core *(Inspired by The Raven by E.A. Poe)* .. 51
- Dylan 54
- Science Test: Invertebrates 56
- Footprints in the Sand 57
- Patriotic Lunch 59
- Boys Life 61

FAMILY 63
- The Keys to All the Power 64
- The Fortunate Child 65
- Stupid Animal Hospital 67
- I'm Finished with Winter 69
- The Flashing *(Home Renovation Haiku)* 71
- Fathers are a Fence 72
- The Seal *(For Ogden Nash)* 74
- Coffee on my Keyboard 75
- Poem for my Gran 76
- Forgotten Key 78
- Neurotypical 79
- Happy Birthday Mom 81
- Paleo Shopping List 83
- Fall Haiku 85

About the Author 87

MOM

Ode to Chores

When the Good Lord
In his wisdom, Hark!
Said "Separate
the light from dark."

He surely didn't
See that time
Would be a scarce
Resource to find

I throw my clothes-wash
In by person
Lest my crazed
Schedule worsen

If I did dark
Then later light
Lord knows I'd be
Doing wash all night

Now let's take a
Look at dishes
Yes! I want to
Save the fishes

But if the washer
Doesn't run
Each night the mornings
Won't be fun

There will be no
Little spoons I trust
And everyone
Will miss the bus

And who is it
Who said that,
If we bought
A tabby cat

They would surely
Clean the litter
A chore which leaves me
Slightly bitter

Now babies
While they make a mess
Their culinary
In-ter-ests

Are simple
Older kids not so
They complicate things
As they grow

Till no meal happens
By the book
Less dinner – more
Short order cook

One says too sweet
One says no crust
One spits it out
With disgust

And if you find
A way to wrangle
Your whole brood
To the table

One eats fast
The other slow
Everyone answers
"I dunno"

Lordy what's a mom to do
With such a cantankerous crew?

But I digress
Our topic here
Is what to do
With soccer gear

Piles of cleats
Sticks lacrosse
And other sporty
Stuff to toss

But instead
I make a bin
Label it
And throw stuff in

So take a cue
From my girl Eve
If you feel a sudden
Pull to leave

You're not at all
The only one
Chores are simply
Not that fun.

Mom Interrupted

When I sit down to write a song
Or read a book you come along
And ask for just a little help
With numbers, letters, or the like

Being kind and some say wise
For a person of my years and size
I set down my hopes and dreams
And tend to yours
For you are just a little tyke

While my creations come and go
(You are the best of them you know)
Like children running to and fro
I chase down words and thoughts that stray

But just as things begin to click
There you are feeling sick
And need to gently lie
Upon my lap and gently cry
And there I stay
Until you wander on your way

Then somehow it's half past noon!
Dinner plans are needed soon
So while my words pull at my sleeve
The half-writ page I have to leave

I quickly clear the breakfast mess

Sort the dishes and the rest
Find some chicken to sauté
Pre-cut carrots save the day
Return with ease
Fingers back down on the keys

What was that thought so pure of heart
That took me to a world apart
I close my eyes to think it through
Instead see all I have to do
Clear my thoughts
Try to ignore
A UPS guy at the door

I hear the school bus on our street
A backpack dragging at his feet
Your brother tells me of his day
Filled with laughter and defeat

And tragic middle school deceit

The dog brings her shredded toy
Pushes it against my knee
Snacks and dinner
A lost shoe
Science homework
Glitter glue

By now I've quite forgotten
My essayist endeavors
By this hour
I'm too tired
To remember why
I was inspired

Pale Pink House Haiku

A pale pink farmhouse
Just passed Applebutter Lane
Art class day again

Middle Age

When dying your hair is less about
 self-expression
And more about self-preservation

When you can make Grandma's cookies
From scratch without a recipe

When you need reading glasses
To text emojis to your children

When you go out for a run
And return with plantar fasciitis

When your significant other blows up
And you don't

When your 12-year old son
Asserts his manhood over the remote

When midnight sounds late

When your morning reflection
Looks more like your mom than yourself

When you lay awake dwelling on
Love and fear for your past and your future

When you have forged root strength
Are as wise as you are strong

When you are clear as a still sea
And open as the Midwest sky

And when finally
You get that extra set of readers for the car

Valentine's Day

Today,
I raise a glass
To coffee in bed

Candlelight dinners
Poems we read

To the martyrdom
Of poor St. Valentine

How did this once
Sweet sonnet rhyme
This lovely waxy taper

Transform itself for tiny hands
Into cards on *Hello Kitty* paper

Sparkle-crafting
School mailboxes

Out of child-size-5
Stride Rite shoeboxes

The teacher's bell
Calls each name
Emma, Jacob, and Cobain
Every student in the class
We wrote each one a card
Alas!

How it gobbled up
The romance and
The soft petalled rose

Chocolate dipped
Strawberries
And the sweet red wine

Here's to you
My Valentine

Tread Lightly Through That Fountain of Youth

We don't know
At the start
That being mom
Is a crucial part

Of the rollout of
Somebody's life
Their every day
And their every night

Like rain we nurture
But soak
With words we praise
But also shatter

Like light we illuminate a matter
But at times shine too brightly
And obscure the point
However slightly

As the north star does
We show the way
Like a cloudy night
Lead our kids astray

And let's not forget
Our goal is to find
A way for our kids

To leave us behind
So tread lightly
Lead with a question
Generally, stay away
From correction

Don't go on about
Wisdom and truth
And err on the side
Of the fountain of youth

Let them fail
And let them win
And one day
They might let you in

Today, I Shouldered Distance

Today, I shouldered distance
Not a lot
A few small inches
Maybe two thumbs
But there it was
My fading eyes
The road turned
My youth an echo
As I pulled back
The box
With its tiny
Ingredients
Wondering why
Did they print them
So small?

Today, I shouldered distance
The great divide
Between who I was
And who I am
A girl of wonder
To a woman of wisdom
The sweet flower of
Patience
Blooms in my heart

Today, I shouldered distance
Nuzzled in my lap
Book after book

Song after song
My son stands
Now eye to eye
My match in
Wit and strength
A gaze
More man
Less Child

Today, I shouldered distance
Haltingly to my door
My mother's gait
Is measured
An heirloom watch spring
Slow to winding
With an eye to resting

   While I gather

   And churn

   Dip wax

   Float lanterns

   Sort clothes

   Mix cumin and coriander

Today, I shoulder
The distance of
My Great
Grandmother's
Sweat and light

And my future
Great
Grandchildren's
Laughter

Today

I have the strength

I hold the space

I am the bridge

And the wide open river

Dirty Socks

I walked passed socks
Left on the floor
Today, and
The day before

Why won't someone
Pick them up?
Are they waiting for a
Sweeper truck?

For the first time ever

It occurs to me
Although I hold an
Advanced degree

I'm the one
Who cleans the mess
Cleans the bathroom
Floor debris

It's me who cleans
The fireplace ash
And Tuesday night
Takes out the trash

Removes hair clogs
From the drain
Walks the puppy

In the rain

(This job description
Is insane)

I'm the one who
Turns off lights
Makes all the meals
Breaks up fights

Really does no one care
The dirty socks are sitting there

Why won't someone
Pick them up

Why didn't I
See before

I'm the one
I'm waiting for

Day Lily

I have great respect
For the flower that blooms
Just once in a season
For one afternoon

And I know first hand
How this flower must feel
To hold to a moment
So sweet, so ideal

As when time stands still
From high on a stage
When life lets you fly
Like a bird from a cage

Think of the lily
Who soaks up the sun
For just a few hours
And then she is gone

But consider,
If a year were a day
And we found a small flower
To bloom in this way

We could have that moment
So rare and so true
If we just stopped to notice
How often we do

Mom Agrees to a Pet

Mom, would you
Agree to a pet?
If I walked it
And loved it
And washed it
And brushed it?

Someone to love
Hug every day
Feed and care for
In every way?

                         A pet? Hmmmm....
                         Why would I agree?
                         We know exactly whose
                         Chore it will be!

                         Darling a guppy
                         Needs a clean tank

                         A kitten has claws
                         That clatter and clank

                         Turtles crawl through
                         The house in a diaper

                         No way I'm getting
                         A mouse eating viper!

                              A billie goat
                       Would eat half the shed
                          Ferrets hide all day
                             Under the bed

                      Remember what happened
                        To poor old Aunt Callie

                         Who took in that stray
                         She found in the alley

                   It chewed all the legs off her
                            Dining room table!

                   Now they eat with the ponies
                       Out back in the stable

What about getting
A pot-bellied pig?

Or an Indian python
-Until it gets big-

You may not believe me
But some folks prefer

Tarantula legs
To the feeling of fur

                          Darling, I don't think you
                                Realize, by golly

                           A hundred-pound Collie
                             Will rip baby's dolly!

If we get a cat
Can I call her Miss Patches?

                      Known by her nickname
                      "Miss Furniture Scratches"

If we get a poodle
You said they don't shed

                      They need to be fed
                      And sleep on the bed!

Puppies are soft
And snuggly and sweet

They give you a paw
If you give them a treat

I'll teach her cool tricks
She'll eat every crumb

That falls to the floor
When dinner is done...

                Mom just stood there
                Refusing to blink
                So quiet I heard
                A drip from the sink.

                Then she shook her head "No"
                But her eyes twinkled "Yes"
                And I think she muttered
                Oh no, what a mess...

Then we tumbled with joy
Into the car
Mom found a place
That wasn't too far

That's where we found
Our very own pup
With an ear that goes down
And the other one up

She's a very good girl
(Only chewed on one shoe)
I do most of the work
But Mom helps a bit too

She plays tug-o-war socks
And chase-with-a-ball

She's the

Snuggliest

Sweetest

Doggie of all!!

Time Stream

For me
Time passing
Like a stream
Faster than you think

I tell myself
I have time
I tell myself
I can start my life
Again

And again

I tell myself
It's not going
To end

My heart feels
To beat on and on
Forever and
Another, one more
Just around the
Corner
After this
Next

I find myself
Lying on the
Dry grass

Staring up
At dinosaur clouds
An endless day
Lying to myself

Slowly I can see
It's just a cloud
It's not a pterodactyl

Time
Like a stream
I step into
And it's gone

Terra Madre

My home
My terra madre
Was a moving castle
Suburban vagabond
Drawing from
My nomadic
Ancestors
Saddling camels
Covered in dust
Through extremes
Of desert life

Harsh day after
Harsh night
I grasped at
The challenge
The breaking
The chaos

Conflict assured
An ever changing
Landscape

Lack of stability
Became
My only mother
The only thing
I could trust
A good fight

Never failed
To deliver

Where soft
Words of support
Gave way to a
Prickly sadness
Again and again and again

Our house
A broken pile of straw
We were the first pig
We ate poison apples
For breakfast lunch and dinner`

My inner snow white
Laced up her combat boots
And went in search of
Hard working dwarves
Forests with empathy
Carved in their trunks

There was no Prince
Save the one with the
Red Corvette
Unapologetic
Swathed in
Smokey stage light
Limitless empyrean
Soul holding
The cold microphone
Against the dissonance
Of feedback

I jumped through
That rabbit hole
Remembering
My child-self
Testing
Curbside balance beams
Testing
Dangerous strangers
I laughed
Dancing across
Burnt out rooftops
Seeking equilibrium
In motion

Late nights
Surrounding me
City sounds
Like distant
Cello strings
Carried under doors
And through cracks
In the walls
Surrounding the
Wooden table
By the window

The writing pencil's
Smooth grip
A conduit
To lost soft
Words of support
I'm Here.
You're OK.
Washed over me

Like rain-soaked
Summer clothes
Lay rest in my bones

Sweater Weather

Yesterday
Geese took flight
Left a winsome
Shallow light

I felt the
Dampness
On the breeze
As I slept
That starry night

When days grow short
I hear my mom
Say "honey,
Put a sweater on"

I see myself
As I was then
Not quite grown
Maybe 10

Old enough to
Braid my hair
Make grilled cheese
Sweep the stair

"No," was always
My reply
Simply said
I was not cold

Mother thought
Sweaters start
When the leaves
Turn red and gold

The Rhetorical Housewife

Why so much toothpaste on the bathroom sink

Why so much poop in the litterbox, stink

Why so many socks scattered hither and yon

Why so much gray to be covered with blonde

The Whole of Me

The man in me
Is wicked strong
Disarmingly smart

Writes important policy
Leads with steadfast dignity

The man in me
Is like the sky

Broad and open
Never shy

The woman in me
Is shelter

Her strength
Is like a bow

Agile and powerful
Yet gentle as a doe

When the two ally
Cast their lots as one

The whole of me rises
Like the morning sun

The Movie of My Life

In the movie of my life
my shoulders are
always down
my back is
always straight

In the movie of my life
I can chop vegetables
really fast
I'm never late and
I'm never sorry
because I always
do the right thing

In the movie of my life
I'm not famous
I'm just well loved
My words never falter
My friends are always by my side

In the movie of my life
you are my champion
and my muse
you never have to remind me
that every moment
is a building block
to the arc of my time here

In the movie of my life
I am inexplicably drawn to
good fortune
good timing
and good people
In the movie of my life
I sketch like Picasso
I design like da Vinci
I fly like Earhart
I cook like Childs
I dance like Tharp
I sing like Fitzgerald

In my movie
the sunsets are vivid
the stars
blanket the sky
on warm summer evenings
my kids
slam screen doors
catch fireflies
wonder
and wander
distracted
by laughter
our dog
eats the cornbread
when no one
is looking
....in the movie of my life.

KIDS

Reluctant Reader

You say you hate to read
But Oh!

You cannot know my darling boy
What future woe and future joy

May delight you if you look
Into the pages of a book

Perhaps a cunning patch and hook
Or a hat that's been mistook

A Shakespeare play
A castaway
A well-dressed hero saves the day

Space age battles fought through time
A small French girl named Madeline

Sir Robins and Fair Guineveres
Tragic tales that end in tears

Who-done-its, and
How-to-do-its
Others you just can't-get-through-its

A deft Haiku of untold passion
Encyclopedias of fashion

Gentle giants
Vicious raptors
Eaten in the final chapters

Reading isn't just for school
Stories love to break the rules

If you never learn to read my friend
You won't know how the story ends

Marvel Heroes

      marvel heroes

  scaling walls

      breaking rules

  making noise

          what it means

        to be boys

Art Collector

Rembrandt liked to paint things darkly
Spreading light on sitters softly
Cracking Roman ceilings show
The patience of Michelangelo

One mustn't go far to convince me
The greatness of Leo DaVinci
From the ballerinas of Renoir
To Edward Hopper's diner bar

The artists to whom I give acclaim
Aren't tinted by fortune nor by fame
My taste for hue and charcoal line
Are not by critic or museum defined

My walls and closets overflow
With flowers of spring and flakes of snow
Works of pencil, crayon, and clay
Surpass the lilies of Monet

Monsters of a thousand teeth
Rubbings of an autumn leaf
Works which stand to tell the tale
Of a giant squid wrapped 'round a whale
Or a spiky parasaurolophus' tail

Mine is a collection of the heart
Priceless, in the world of art

For the Love of Pete!
(Stop Rocking on the Chair)

Stop rocking on the chair
Eat your dinner

Stop rocking on the chair
I'm sorry you don't like peas

Stop - rocking - on – the - chair
How many times do I have to tell you
Woah! Easy with the ketchup Mister

Hey, stop rocking on the chair
It's going to break
It loosens the wood
That's how the other chairs broke
Someone pass the fries, please?

Seriously, stop rocking
No soda we just have water

Oh, for the love of Pete
Stop rocking back!
Crud, now you fell over
Are you OK?
Come back to the table

Feet off the table!
Yes
You can be excused

Soccer Haiku

Balled up soccer socks
Outside the laundry basket
First signs of autumn

What They Don't Tell You

They don't tell you
   the house
   will be covered
   in jam

That you won't get
   a good night's
   sleep for a decade

The baby shower
   was all smiles
   and love

Blankets
   so soft
Plush toys
   so sweet

A send-off to start
   a 10-year retreat

It's not till you're home
   with the baby in tow
   when you suddenly see

The soft blankets
   the toys, the books and
   the crib and think
   to yourself

It's not for me

It's not mine at all

It's meant for the
   monkey just down
   the hall

The little bean
   taking up space

In what
   once was the office
   but now it's their place

The baby's address
   and mine are the same

...It has even taken
   my last name

They don't tell you
   for the next
   6 to10 years

Small people will
   break everything
   fragile

Throw their food

Draw on the walls

Scream when they
   don't get their way

But for some
   sweet reason
   we want them
   to stay

Little Toes

Butterflies
Tiny wings
Tiny toes

Movement
Our first
Conversation

Late at night
The town
Asleep

You would tap
On the window
Of my belly

Pulling the strings
Of my heart

Were you
Checking to see
If I was still there

To be sure
You were not alone

To say softly
You wanted to play

My belly grew
Huge and tight
You were busy

In your tiny den
I pressed softly
Against your little hands

Or were they feet?
Or were they feet?

Little Toes II

Aww... little toes
So so cute
Look at the little baby toes
They are soooo cute

The puppy is licking them
And now they're in baby's mouth
Maybe that's not a good idea

Splash little toes
Warm soapy water

All cleaned up

Roy G Biv

Red is for racing to save small kittens from tall trees

Orange is for roasting the seeds and cutting out a face

Yellow is for making squiggly lines on a hot dog

Green is for garden snakes to hide in

Blue is for diving into when you're hot

Indigo is to see the stars sparkle against

Violet is for picking the best ones and making mom smile

Common Core
(Inspired by The Raven by E.A. Poe)

Once upon a school board meeting,
While I jotted notes, half sleeping,
Over many a quaint and curious
Bylaw which had come before.

While I nodded, nearly napping
Suddenly there came a clapping
Applause for a complete re-mapping
Of the educational decor.

   "*'Tis a fad*," I muttered,
   "Two plus two still equals four"
      Quoth Miss Watkins... *Common Core*

Ah, distinctly I remember,
It was in the bleak November;
When a new administration
Was elected to the fore

The fate of every state entwined
By No Child Left Behind
Our resources we could combine
Improve on what has come before
Create a standardized equation
Which the bureaucrats adore!

   Nameless here for evermore
      Quoth Miss Watkins... *Common Core*

U.S. scores continued falling,
"A state standard!" was the calling
A better way to measure,
quantify, assess, and score.

From California to Maine
Make the standards look the same!
Day by day, to still the beating,
Of my heart I stood repeating

    "Two plus two still equals four"
    "Two plus two still equals four"
      This it is and nothing more

Create a race with every school!
Test them on the golden rule!
School shelves burst to overflowing
Pearson resources galore.

So that now to fill the coffers
Of the top publishing authors
A new textbook hand delivered
To each student shore to shore

And with every test comprised
Of questions now all standardized
Just one book from shore to shore
    Quoth Miss Watkins... *Common Core*

Suddenly I heard a tapping,
Ticonderoga pencils snapping
Back into the schoolhouse turning
Computers all accounted for

Every teacher worst to best
Was now teaching to the test
A growing feeling of unrest
Knocking on each schoolhouse door.

Every teacher worst to best
Was now teaching to the test
Who? I stammered wins this race?
Answer please i do implore!

    Quoth Miss Watkins... *Common Core*
    Quoth Miss Watkins... *Common Core*

Dylan

Boy of the sea
He's fast and free
Let's his hair go wild

Although quite quick
To swing a stick
His demeanor is quite mild

At the age of one
The cats would run
He squoze them way too tight

But now they come
When day is done
To sleep with him each night.

A trumpet-eer
A well-trained ear
He rocks and he can roll

A jazzy cat
An acrobat
Who no one can control

Stands by his bruv
Gives up the love
Even when they fight

He's sleepy
Every day at school
Then stays up all night!

Science Test: Invertebrates

On the day of the science test
I tried to wake you
You were like a porifera
Still, asymmetrical

I shook your shoulder
And like a gastropod
You crawled out of bed
Moving ever so slowly
Toward the shower

I quizzed you over breakfast
You have always had
The impressive memory and vision
Of a cephalopod

You were hydrostatic when I said
There were linked sections of sausage
Frying in the pan.
The dog clung to me
Like a leech, hoping they'd
Fall into her domain

The bus pulled up, its radial tires
Screeching to a halt like a
Stinging-celled cnidarian.
I waved and said,
"Good luck on your science test!"

Footprints in the Sand

The retreating
Shoreline
As we drive
Sun-soaked
Windblown
Sand in our shoes

I see the baby
Growing faint in
The memory glass
Fading sunrise
Over crashing waves

I see an echo
The top step
Tiny hands reaching
Your voice calling
"I carry you!"

I lift you
Little sack of potatoes
Trot you downstairs
On my hip

I see you
Waving
Your dad heading off
To work
You give him

Fair warning
"Watch out for rhinos"

I see you
Same bright eyes
Summer freckles
Winsome smile

A touch of
Wisdom in your eyes
13 times
Around the sun

Thousands of shells
Washed up on the beach
And carried back out to sea
Our footprints
In the sand

Patriotic Lunch

Cacophony of
Metal trays
And laughter

Lazy sneakers
Squealing on
Linoleum

Kool Aid
Ham sandwiches
Uneaten bananas
BBQ Lays and
Chocolate Moo

Ranch Doritos
Nacho Cheese
Cool Ranch
Taco
Toasted Corn
Spicy Sweet Chili
Fiery Habanero
Blazin' Buffalo

And worn down
Lunch ladies
Patrolling the room
Like prison guards
Lunchable sentries

Holding back
The chaos and the din
The last gate
Between order and
Anarchy

And there against the
Painted beige cinderblock

Floating above the braids
Above the paisley
Lunchboxes
Above the crew cut boys
And their Spiderman
Water bottles

Waving
In the air-vent breeze
Bathed
In fluorescent
Lunchroom light

Our American flag

Boys Life

smelly dog
grungy paws
muddy sheets
the boys
up late

cat hotels
pillow forts
rainbow fish
pancake stacks
loaded nachos

dirty dishes
bike rides
sun burns
band aids
wrestling matches

go fishes
dump trucks
lake kayaks
firepit marshmallows
lego ships

state parks
mine crafts
mom hugs
beef jerky
frisbee golf

head lamps
capture flags
make friends
lose socks
sword sticks

movie nights
food fights
hot chocolate
jumping spiders
water striders

FAMILY

The Keys to All the Power

The first one in the shower
Holds the keys to all the power

For this citizen decides
To be benevolent or cruel

Will his reign be one of mercy
A regime of law and rule

Or will a dearth of heated water
Go down the drain with his endeavor

To be clean as a whistle
Pray he settles for some gristle

Behind a little toe
Or a left or right side ear

For a benevolent commander
In the shower won't meander

He believes that others aught
To have some water that is hot!

The Fortunate Child

The fortunate child
Is flanked by love
Both from within
And from above

Parents who
Care deeply for
One another
At their core

Give the gift
Of happiness
To their child
Through every bliss

The coffee that
He pours for she
The special note
She leaves for he

These gestures
Circle through
For kindness is
As kindness do

Meanders to
A child's true
Nature and their
Nurture too

Tape reminders
To the door
Give your person
Every day

A violet
A cup of joe
An amulet
A simple poem
A book
A hug
An atta boy
Fill your home
With love and joy

Stupid Animal Hospital

There's a place
Here
I dislike more
Than any other

It's where we went
When Tika died

It's where we went
When Gracie was
   hit by a car

And I've just left
Colby
My handsome Tabby
   in their care

A place which raises
Uncomfortable
Questions

About a life

The value of
My own existential
   existence

Before I left
I gave him a pep talk
He looked
Scared and tired

I said "Meow"
But I don't know if
I got the words right

I'm Finished with Winter

I'm finished with winter
I'm ready to shed these
Cumbersome coats
And layers and gloves

Dirty salt crusted onto the car
Brushing off on all our clothes
I'm finished with bad tomatoes
Anemic cucumbers

Shuffling in slippers
Wrapped in sweaters
Lingering near the fireplace
Our snowman a frozen lump

I'm ready for grassy
Sundays spent knee high
In the river fishing for
Smooth flat jumping stones

Wild forest trails flanked
By fallen logs, you and
Your brother chasing
Uncatchable chipmunks

Catching our breath in
Doorways, running
From sudden summer
Storm drenched, still warm

Stabbing airholes
With kitchen knives into
Perfectly good Tupperware
For crayfish and toads

I'm ready for herbs on the deck
Late night bonfires
Marshmallow torches
And sweet lemonade
On wide front porches

The Flashing
(Home Renovation Haiku)

behold the flashing
whisking away summer rain
basement dry again

Fathers are a Fence

Fathers are a fence
You climb over
Hang around on
Lean on when you're tired
Perch on in fair weather
Use to check your balance
Will not fall or break
No matter where you wander
Or how big a mistake
Fathers are there
When you return
In disrepair
And set their coffee
On the porch
Or pull up the old porch chair
And wait quietly
For words
You shuffle feet and stare
A father is a mountain
Sturdy as a bear
Stoic and heroic
Tells it to you straight
A shoulder you can cry on
Shoes that you can try on
Someone you can love
And someone you can hate

Fathers are a fence
You climb over

Hang around on
Hold to keep you steady
Will not fall or break
Teach you to be reckless
Teach you to be kind
Lift you up so you can see
A father is the man
One day you will be

The Seal
(For Ogden Nash)

Playful and sweet
The pet I find ideal

My perfect companion
Is undoubtedly the seal

Though earless
They're not hearless

Fond of sledding
Never shedding

Coffee on my Keyboard

Café Bustello
Early morning
Cinnamon galaxy
Swirling
Frothy white

Mug warming
Cold palms
Pellet stove
Heats my flank
All asleep
All quiet

I set down to write
Considering words
A blank digital page
Weighing thoughts
Warming
Cold hands
Wide mug

Barley Patches
Tail a-wag
One swift nudge
Wet happy nose
My trusty dog
And the perfect latte
Wipe out my MacBook Pro

Poem for my Gran

The bathroom smelled of
   rose Dove
"Sit here hon," she taps the pink
   vinyl cushion
Two small chairs and a
   folding table
In her tiny North Bergen
   kitchen

She closes my soft fingers
With her rough life hands
Pressing two folded dollars
   into my palm
She whispers, "Don't tell
   your grandfather"

A world of opera, the beauty parlor,
   and fear
Don't sit there, take off your shoes,
   you're too *thin* dear
Thin,
   auburn curls,
   and a perpetual falling
   bra strap

They say she was a great singer in her day
They say she sewed in a sweatshop
That her mother died when she was a child

They say her father was cruel;
   a crusher of dreams

On that cellular wind
I caught your joy and sorrow
Carried past your life
And far across your DNA

Thank you, Gran
For the love of song
And the gift of music
It was far more than you
Ever could have imagined
   to give

Forgotten Key

When the bus pulled in
Close to midnight

Returning from the city
To the frigid winter of Bethlehem

Cold, like the cold shoulder of
The Pennsylvania Dutch

The phone rang in our little house
Just six miles down the snowy highway

Me and the boys awaiting your return
Your voice tired not wanting to ask

That little metal key, the key to your car
Resting patiently on your desk

Eighty-nine miles east, in New York City
Wondering why it was there

But I was happy to come
And rescue you in the cold

The little key's twin sister in my pocket
Driving through the snow

Late in the night
To take you home

Neurotypical

ADHD
OCD
Depression
Bi-Polar
Autistic
Central
Processing
Consult
Teachers
Doctors
Infer
Confer
Drive to
The next
Meeting
School
Kids Peace
Drop him somewhere
On the spectrum
They see a graph
A syndrome
Set up a 504
Create an IEP
They don't see
My kid
Wicked funny
Wicked smart
Who can sing
In a British accent

Throw a baseball
Clear across the road
Into Angela's yard
You keep trying
To make him learn
The way you learn
The way you think
It is just so neurotypical
Of you to try to make
The world in your
Own image
But your image
Is our creation
We are the special
Needs kids who
Landed on the Moon
Wrote the 5th Symphony
Ruled England
Painted the Sistine Chapel
Led America through the Civil War
Invented Calculus
Painted Starry Night
Wrote War and Peace
Won the Nobel Prize in Economics
Developed the theory of evolution

You play in our sandbox
...and walk in our dreams

Happy Birthday Mom

On my first day
All was new
My only knowing
Was of you

Your voice
Your touch
Your blood and bone
All of this was my home

50 years have passed
Since then
My foil and
My heroine

Having danced
Among the stars
And likewise stumbled
Home from bars

With crows nest's
Spyglass clarity
In all directions
Open sea

I use the compass
In my heart
A gift you gave me
At the start

To steady on
Power through
Still my thoughts
Sense what's true

Happy birthday
Mom
To you

Paleo Shopping List

Black Forest Bacon
    From the chilled case
    Not from the Black Forest

Pastured eggs
    From happy chickens
    Pecking at bugs and bits of grain

Cashews, salted
    Sent by barge along
    The Mekong River
    Of Viet Nam

Potatoes for mash
    Hoed by the
    Calloused hands of an
    Idaho farmer

Kerry Gold
    So we can eat
    the grassy fields
    and the Irish sun
    Deep in the cells
    Of our Celtic Butter

Avocados, tomatoes, and onions
    For guacamole
    Ripened under blue skies
    Of the rolling Chilean hillsides

Brussels sprouts
    Grown on a Pennsylvania
    Farm, trucked in by the case
    Wrapped in little nets

French water
    In glass bottles
    Mineralized by the
    Stones of a French
    Mountain creek bed

Neanderthal strength

Carboniferous oxygen

Pangaean worldview

Fall Haiku

School supplies piled high
On the dining room table
One last summer swim

About the Author

Brenda Kahn is a poet, memoirist and an international recording artist who has shared the stage with Bob Dylan, David Byrne and Jeff Buckley. She has expertise in changing both guitar strings and diapers. She is a writer of songs, poetry, memoir, and excuse notes for sick kids. She can paint and spackle like nobody's business and will also perform a cover of Bessie Smith's *Ain't Nobody's Business* if you request it at a live show. She lives in South Salem, NY with her husband and two boys, her golden retriever (Barley Patches), her two cats (Fluffy and Colby) and Ekko the crested gecko.

Learn more about Bren at www.brendakahn.com

Stay connected and support her work at www.patreon.com/brendakahn

www.ingramcontent.com/pod-product-compliance
Lightning Source LLC
Chambersburg PA
CBHW020429010526
44118CB00010B/485